THE LIQUOR KING OF THE BLUE RIDGE AND OTHER STORIES OF AHO

BY

ROY ELLIS WEAVER

Roy E Weaver

This book is a follow-up to two earlier works by the author about the communities along the Blue Ridge in Watauga County, North Carolina. The earlier books were largely based on oral traditions but this book is based on stories that appeared in the newspapers, mainly the Watauga Democrat and the Lenoir News.

Many of these stories are about people who have been largely forgotten but were important people in our community one hundred years ago. It is my hope that this small book will revive the memory of these people and the contribution they made to our community.

THE OBITUARY LADY

In the rural areas of Watauga County in the years after the Civil War death and burial was a local affair. A local carpenter would build a simple wooden coffin, the men in the community would dig the grave and the local minister would conduct the funeral service. There was no notice in the local papers, unless someone in the community wrote a tribute and sent it to the paper. The Aho community was fortunate that they had Mrs. Jenny Matney Miller who was a master of the style of obituaries that were common in the late Victorian era. Mrs. Miller was the daughter of the legendary minister, James Matney who was one of the early settlers in Aho. She was a leader in founding the Friendship Methodist Church. She was a teacher and received high praise. She taught the school at Deerfield in 1897. On January 18th 1900, the Watauga Democrat had the following article about the Matneys: *"Rev Mr. and Mrs. Matney celebrated their golden wedding on Wednesday, January the 10th. They, having been married fifty years on that day, are getting up in years; yet seem jolly and full of life.*

Mr. Matney has labored long for the salvation of souls, and we hope the Lord will spare him yet a good many years to work for the cause of Christ.

Miss Jenny, their daughter, invited a few intimate friends, and gave a nice dinner to honor the event. The table was spread with good things, fruit cake and delicacies in abundance. All seemed to enjoy the occasion very much. We fear that we will soon have to bid adieu to Miss Jenny as she is reflecting on matrimony. We are sorry to give her up but our loss is his gain."

In 1902 Jenny Matney left her home in Aho to teach at a mission school at Bessemer City, North Carolina. A man named John Jones wrote a letter to the Watauga Democrat praising Miss Matney which I will quote in part: "On last Friday the people of this community were highly entertained by the students of the mission school taught by Miss Jenny Mateny of Deerfield in Watauga County.

We are proud of the school and delighted to have in our midst such a teacher. May she live long to be a blessing to the world. The writer is satisfied that Miss Jenny is molding characters to be a blessing to the world and a star in her crown."

Soon after the Watauga Democrat began publishing in 1889 Jenny Matney began to write obituaries for people who died in the Aho community. The first was written about a twelve year old girl who died from a heart condition in December 1890: *"Maggie E. daughter of G. L. and Martha Storie, was born Feb. 15, 1878 and died of heart dropsy, Dec 3, 1890 aged twelve years, nine months and eighteen days. Little Maggie was a very remarkable child and wise beyond her years. At home she was an obedient daughter, a loving sister, and kind and generous to all. During her last illness she suffered a great deal, but was very patient and seemed more anxious for those who waited on her, than for herself: often begging them to rest. Sometime before she died, she told one who was standing by her bed, that she was going to die but said: 'don't tell father, it will trouble him.' The night before she died she became exceedingly happy and her sweet little face beamed with angelic brightness, and she sang 'I am going home to die no more'. To those who stood around her bed she said 'I'm going to live with Jesus and how sweet it will be to clasp the hand of Jesus on the banks of sweet*

Deliverance.'   About an hour before she died she arose from the bed and on being asked what she wanted, said: 'I want to go to father.' Someone took her by the hand and she walked to the bed where her father lay, put her arms around his neck, kissed him twice and walked back to her bed as if nothing was the matter. She left loving messages for all her relatives and seemed very anxious for those who were not religious. She requested her father to write to her uncle who was in the west and tell him to meet her in heaven. Just before she died she called all present to her bedside and told them goodbye and said 'meet me in heaven.'

Yesterday evening her little body was consigned to its last resting place to await the resurrection morn, but the pure spirit has fled to the bosom of the Savior it loved. Free from sin and sorrow, the last pain has been felt and all is joy peace and love."

In May 1892, Miss Matney wrote an obituary for Molly Storie Triplett: *"Molly, the daughter of Jesse and Mary Storie was born March 6, 1869 and was united in matrimony with Granville Triplett September 1, 1886. She professed religion and joined the Baptist church at Laurel Fork March 1887 but soon after removed to Roan Mountain, Tennessee where she remained a constant member of the Baptist church at that place until her death which occurred on April, 18, 1892. From the first of her sickness she told her friends that she would not recover but she was ready for death. She had no anxiety about her future state but felt all was well. All of her anxiety seemed to be for others especially those of her friends who were unconverted. About 11 pm on the night before she died she called her mother to her bedside and told her that she wanted to tell her how good she felt; that she was perfectly happy and was not suffering from any pain. She continued in this happy frame of mind until the pale messenger came and kissed her pure spirit away."*

In July 1899 Miss Matney wrote the obituary for her aunt, Carolina Matney Hampton: *"Carolina Matney was born in Wilkes County North Carolina June 9, 1826 and departed this life June 15, 1899. At the age of thirty-six years she married Aaron Hampton of Watauga County with whom she lived happily until his death.*
Hers was an exemplary Christian life. Her girlhood was pure and spotless. She was a model wife and mother, and the years of her widowhood were untarnished. She was kind and affectionate to her friends and relatives and always ready to comfort and help the distressed and unfortunate. Her life was one of suffering, but she bore all with meek submission; she never murmured or complained. She lived well and died well. Her last illness was brief only lasting a few hours. A short time before she died she called her loved ones around her, told them she was going to die and had them promise to meet her in heaven. She then committed herself to the hands of God: repeated and tried to sing a portion of the hymn commencing 'Jesus, lover of my soul' and as the sun sank in the western horizon the head that had so often been racked with pain sank on its pillow, the

weary eye lids closed, the faithful bosom ceased to heave and softly and gently as the gathering twilight, the pure spirit took its flight to that beautiful country where sickness and death are strangers where loved ones dwell and Jesus reigns. 'O Death where is thy sting? O grave, where is thy victory?' Thanks be to God who giveth us the victory through our Lord, Jesus Christ."

In the year 1900, Jenny Matney Miller penned another obituary for Mary Bradford Harstin. The name Harstin in largely forgotten in the Aho community but it was a prominent family at that time. Mary's husband G. H. Harstin, was a veteran of the Civil War. He served in the famous 26th North Carolina. He moved to the Aho community sometime after the Civil War. He was instrumental in establishing Friendship Methodist Church. He owned a general store for a period of time. His wife Mary Bradford was ill for a period of time and apparently Mrs. Jenny Matney Miller helped care for her in her final days and sent the following obit to the Watauga Democrat: *"Mary Bradford was born on June 5, 1835 and departed this life on April 25th 1900. When about fifteen years old she embraced religion and joined the Methodist Church and ever after lived a consistent faithful Christian life. She was a devoted wife and the mother of three children, a son and two daughters. Nothing could be more beautiful than her love for her children. No distance was too great to keep her from her children if she thought they needed her assistance. She was faithful to all her friends ready to lend a helping hand in times of need. The sick and unfortunate were her special care. Her last visit was to a sick child. She was loved by all and will be missed by all. For several years her health has been delicate but she bore it with Christian submission and was always cheerful. Although her suffering was great she spent the last night of her life in prayer, and she was often heard to say 'my Jesus, my heaven, my all'. All that affection and medical skills could do for her restoration was done but to no avail. The end came about six o'clock in the morning, and she who had lived nearly sixty-five years and braved the storms of the restless sea of life, laid down the cares of the earth and peacefully passed away to that other and better country where the inhabitants never suffer pain and no funeral processions are ever seen for death cannot enter the pearly gates. The funeral service was conducted by the Rev. James Matney on the morning of April 27th and the beloved form was bourn to its last resting place at a sunny spot near Laurel Fork Baptist Church and committed to the ground: earth to earth, ashes to ashes, dust to dust. 'O that awful sound, once heard never forgotten the falling of the clods on the coffin lid.*

With tear stained eyes we have gazed on the mortal remains of our dear friend. When we behold her again she will be clothed with immortality and we shall see with immortal eyes. With sad heart we shall say goodbye but not forever. We shall meet again. Death is only a transfer, the gateway of entrance to our father's house, where our loved ones bash in the unfading beams of the endless summer land and where songs of gladness wait our coming home. To the bereaved husband, the motherless children, and hosts of friends and relatives we extend deep and earnest sympathy and pray for them the sustaining grace of God in their sore bereavement."

Mr. G. H. Harstin survived his wife by sixteen years and died at the home of his daughter, Mrs. Shull in 1916.

In May 1902 Jenny Matney Miller wrote another obituary of a child in the Aho area"

At 5 o'clock in the morning of May 1st the pale angel Death rowed his phantom boat across the mystic river, entered the happy home of Mr. and Mrs. N. N. Ford and kissed away the pure spirit of little Eva Mae, the only child in the home.

Her stay on earth was a brief one, only two years three months and two days, yet brief as it was, the little form had twined itself around the hearts of those who knew and loved her, and the home will seem desolate and lonely without the childish prattle of little Mae. Sometimes we wonder why it is that those tender buds are torn from the parent tree when they are being cultivated with such care; but somewhere in the eternal summer land our heavenly father has a place to plant them where they will bloom in fadeless beauty never to be nipped by the frost of care or sorrow. How fitting that just as beauteous spring was awakening all nature into life and the morning bursting forth in splendor, little Mae was called away to the home where winter winds never blow and darkness cannot enter. We sympathize with the bereaved parents whose home has been thrice left childless by the relentless hand of death but would console them with the fact that if they are true to the Master they will meet their darling again, for He who has provided a balmy south for the summer birds to which they fly intuitively, with blind hope and trust, has provided a shelter for us where we may meet the loved and lost, *and realize our soul's dream.*

Yes, over the lonely, over the unknown sea we call death; he will guide us safely to a haven to a home immortal not made with human hands eternal in the heavens."

Only a week later there was another death of a child in Aho. Joe and Hester Greene lived near Laurel Fork Church. Their only son, Ronda Blackburn died and again Jenny Matney Miller wrote another eloquent tribute: "*Again that never welcome guest, Death has entered a peaceful happy home, broken the family circle, and borne away the pet of the household.*

On the morning of May 7, the spirit of little Ronda Blackburn, the only son of Mr. and Mrs. Joseph Greene took its flight and silently passed into that shadowy land which to us is shrouded in mystery, for from its shore no one returns to tell us what lies beyond.

God lent little Ronda to his fond parents only a short time three years, four months and three days, but the little life was full of sunshine. All who knew him loved him.

During his last illness his suffering was intense but he bore it with a patience seldom manifested by persons of mature years. He has left a grief stricken home but he has passed into a house of many mansions and forms golden link to the chain which binds the sorrowing relatives to the glory land.

Jenny Miller wrote another obituary in 1912 about the death of her neighbor Sophia Triplett Greene: *Sophia Ann, daughter of Jesse and Caroline Triplett was born March 1, 1894 and passed to life eternal on October 21, 1912. She was married to Bynum Greene on April 15, 1910. A few days after her marriage, she was converted and joined the Baptist church at Laurel Fork and was a constant member until her death. Her illness was brief but her suffering was intense. Yet, she bore it all with a patience resignation that is seldom seen in one so young. She showed no fear of death and talked cheerfully of her departure as she would of visiting a dear friend.*

A few hours before her death, she turned to her devoted young husband who was weeping at her bedside and asked him to meet her in heaven.

In penning this little sketch, we tell the same story that is daily being told, of a fond father and mother bereft of a loving daughter, the pet of a household, of a husband weeping because there was no fond wife at his side, of affectionate brothers and sisters whose hearts are sore because a much loved sister walks with them no more, saddest of all, of a sweet little babe who will never know a mother's love or feel the gentle touch of a mother's hand. O! Death thou art inexorable, thou touch means tears and heartaches. No wonder thou are never a welcome guest. But death the king of terror as he is to a large part of our race is not the monster that he seems. Death, the huge black winged angel who has been for six thousand years perpetually hovering over our earth casting his dark shadow at every household and into every heart. Death has one office to perform for us and one only to break the shell that shuts us up in the little dark prison of earthly life and allow the soul to unfold its golden pinions and soar out into a broader world and free to shout with one of old, O death where is thy sting? The family of the deceased extends their heartfelt thanks to their friends and neighbors."

It was almost two years later that a sister of Sophia Greene died and Jenny Miller penned another obituary: "*It is with a sad heart that we note the death of Mrs. Catherine Greene, wife of Hardin Greene and daughter of Jesse and Caroline Triplett. She was born in 1885 and died in March 1914 age 28 years. She professed faith in Christ and joined the Methodist Episcopal Church when a girl and lived a devoted Christian life until death. She was married to Hardin Greene in 1908 and to the union was born three children one boy and two girls. One girl died before her mother and is now awaiting her coming. Her suffering was great but she bore it with patience. Three doctors were summoned and everything was done for her relief but to no avail as our heavenly father saw fit to take her home to rest. It was her request on Sunday morning before she died on Thursday that they sing the song that her sister was heard repeating before her death (No Sorrow Will Be There). After the song she asked her sister if she heard the singing up there. She said it was sweeter singing than they could do. Then she turned to her father and asked 'where is Mr. Payne?' She said she would like to hear him pray once more and at her request the minister came and in a low weak voice she asked him to pray again which he did. Her husband was called to her bed, and she told him to stay with her while he could and to meet her in heaven. On Thursday about noon she quietly, peacefully fell to sleep in the arms of Jesus.*

The funeral was held at Laurel Fork on Saturday conducted by Rev. Payne."

All though it was signed only with a D which probably meant daughter, the obituary of James P. Matney was in all probability written by Jenny Miller: " *James P. Matney was born in Transylvania County Virginia on July 5, 1822, but before he had grown to manhood his father brought his family to North Carolina and settled in Moravian Falls in Wilkes County. He was married to Myra Wells on January 10th 1850. Of this union was born seven children were. Three proceeded their father to the glory land.*

He professed religion when a small boy and joined the Methodist Episcopal church. He was licensed to exhort when quiet a young man and officiated in the church as was licensed to preach. Shortly afterward he moved his family to Washington County, Tennessee. In 1872 he entered the itinerancy in the Blue Ridge Atlantic Conference and traveled until he became too old and feeble to bear the fatigue of church work. He was always faithful to his charge and sacrificed his time and other interests to the church and the cause of the Master. He preached a religion of purity and he practiced it all his life.

During the last years of his life he suffered a great deal but bore it with meek submission and Christian fortitude. For some time before he died he seemed to feel that his work on earth was done. He was expecting the summons home and he talked a great deal about his departure. A day or two before he died he asked his grandson to go to the organ and play and sing. He selected a number of songs and after they were sung, he said that it seemed like his children who had died were smiling upon him: that they had never seemed so near.

At 10 o'clock on the morning of February 28 while sitting in his chair by the fireside the messenger came and the immortal spirit, blood washed and glory lit took it flight the home of many mansions.

Our hearts are sore from the severing of the ties that are so binding but we sorrow not as those who have no hope for we know that he fought a good fight and kept the faith and henceforth there is laid up for his a crown of righteousness and I doubt not that it will be resplendent with many stars."

The last obituary by Jenny Miller was written in January 1917 and was a short obituary of a small child. "Death entered the home of Milton Storie on December 29th and snatched from the embrace of his fond parents little Lonnie Hughes. The little fellow had only been in the home ten weeks, but long enough to entwine himself about the heart of his parents, grandparents and relatives. They will miss little Lonnie but will have the sweet assurance that he has been transplanted into the garden, and somewhere in that beautiful place the sweet budding life will unfold and bloom where the frost of death never nips the bud nor withers the flower"

Mrs. Jenny Miller's health was failing and she was unable to write more obituaries. She died on May 22, 1918 at her home in Aho. There was no one to write an elaborate obituary for her. There was only a short notice in the Watauga Democrat which read: *"The death of Jenny Matney Miller occurred at her home near Aho last Wednesday. Watauga loses one of its most choice ladies. Her illness was long but her suffering was bourn with the Christian fortitude that characterized her daily life. She was buried the following day near the old home."*

Jenny Matney Miller was remembered in her community for many years. Old timers talked of her religious zeal and many years after her death people remember her playing the old pump organ at Friendship Church. Some people believed that on a still day they could still hear her play the old pump organ as she practiced for the Sunday services

OTHER OBITUARIES

Jenny Matney Miller set a high standard for writing obituaries but her nephew, Thomas Hampton was also a master of the Victorian style of obituaries. In April 1909 he wrote the following obituary of Thomas Hall Triplett the patriarch of the Triplett's of Aho: *"Thomas H. Triplett the subject of this sketch was born in Wilkes County March 8th, 1831 and departed this life March 20, 1909.*

On the Sunday following, surrounded by his wife, children and grandchildren, and a large crowd of connections and friends, we laid him to rest in the Friendship M.E. Church burying ground, his pastor the Rev J. M. Payne conducting the service.

He has been a noted character in the Blue Ridge Township, one of the strongest men and best farmers in our section. His Blackburn farm shows what one man with the push and energy he had can do in twenty years. He was a good neighbor and attended strictly to his own business, a kind father and an affectionate husband.

The tears shed at his burying show the respect in which he was held by the people in his settlement.
Death is always an unwelcome visitor. We are never ready for him to come. Those acquainted with Uncle Tom, as the writer always called him, for the last six years would not have been surprised to hear of his death at any time, and yet we were not ready. His wife, his companion for many years did not want to give him up. His grandson and his wife who attended him in his long sickness, don't see how they can do without him.

Uncle Tom is gone; brother is gone, grandfather is gone, father is gone, husband is gone—he has left his earthly home. His place in the home is vacant. We look in the house, on the farm but he is not there. We listen but we cannot hear his voice. He has crossed the dark river; he is done with sickness and sorrow, pain and death. To his wife and children we can only say. It is sweet to look beyond the pilgrimage of life to the eternal city where we hope to meet again."

homas Hall Triplett (1831-1909) and Rachel Stori riplett (1823-1870).

The Underwood family moved from Sampson to a farm below Laurel Fork Baptist. There were few opportunities for young men in Aho. Two of the young men of that family, William and Pink, heard of the opportunities for homesteading in the west left Aho and went to Idaho. Pink's stay is Idaho was short. The Idaho Free Press printed his obituary in November 1897: " *Pink Underwood who has been seriously ill at the home of S. Ingram for the past three weeks took a turn for the worse Monday and died at half past four in the morning. He had typhoid fever but it was thought his naturally robust constitution would tide him over. Everything was done to keep the grim destroyer from taking him but he failed and went to his home beyond as one asleep. William Underwood, a brother, was the only relative here and was with him until the last. Pink had many sterling qualities which endeared him to a legion of friends who mourn his demise. He has a father living near Aho North Carolina and was twenty-nine years old. He intended to visit his old home in North Carolina after proving his homestead. He was buried at Cottonwood Idaho.*"

Two years later in June 1899 Pink Underwood's half-brother, George Storie advertised for sale six acres of land that Pink Underwood owned near Laurel Fork Baptist Church.

Probably the best example of the Victorian obituary was the daughter of Henry Hartley who was born in the Bamboo community: *"Pantha Elizabeth Hartley, daughter of Henry and Delphia Hartley was born on New River on the first day of October 1886. When her father moved his family to Johnson County Tennessee and settled on Mills Creek at the foothills of Stone Mountain, Pantha was a twelve years old, unassuming, modest, beautiful, and bright.*

At a protracted meeting held by Harrison Farthing and David Greene at Pine Grove church, this modest damsel professed faith in Christ. She yielded up her heart to God and her comely form to the liquid wave in Baptism, the sacred rite being administered by Rev. Harrison Farthing. Pantha grew to womanhood and gave her social circle perpetual sunshine and joy. She was noted for her industry, her modesty, her mild and well balanced disposition, and for the strength and purity of her character. She was a model of chastity and virtue. She was married to Fred L. Harman on September 19, 1903. He took his young bride to his home on Cove Creek, Watauga County. They started in new marriage life with hopes buoyant and prospects unusually bright. The next scene is one of deep sadness and melancholy. The Death angel's bony fingers knocked at the door of this new made home and called for the young wife and mother. She obeyed the summon after about forty days of agony and pain upon a bed of affliction which she bore with unprecedented patience and the sweet baby and broken hearted husband

She went away from earth to heaven before she has reached her eighteenth year. A Friend"

On March 25, 1926 the Lenoir Topic has the short obituary of Jesse Storie who was the last living son of the original settler in Aho, John Storie and one of the last veterans of the Civil War in the Blue Ridge Township. *"Jesse Storie died at his home following an illness caused by heart dropsy and was buried the following day at Laurel Fork Cemetery. The funeral service was conducted by Robert Shore and Wesley Ashley. Mr. Storie was in his nineties and was the last charter member of the Laurel Fork Baptist Church. He joined the Baptist faith when he was only sixteen years old and was a devoted member throughout his life. He is survived by his wife and a number of children and grandchildren."*

GEORGE STORIE

When the, author was growing up in the Aho Community he heard competing stories about his great grandfather George Storie. My mother greatly admired her grandfather and told about how he helped needy people and tried to build up the Aho Community. My paternal grandmother hated George Storie and told stories about his drinking and his lack of religious conviction. My father and uncle told stories about the rants and rages of George Store at his community store in Aho.

However there was another side to George Storie that was told in letters he wrote to newspapers and the letters others wrote about him. This chapter tells his story based on his own writings and what others wrote about him.

THE LIQUOR KING OF THE BLUE RIDGE GEORGE STORIE AND THE BATTLE OVER PROHIBITION IN WATAUGA

In the first decade of the 20th century the big political issues was the battle over the sale of alcoholic beverages. There was a national movement for Prohibition led by Woman's Christian Temperance Union (WCTU) and the Anti-Saloon League. In 1908 the state of North Carolina scheduled a up or down vote on Prohibition for May 1908. Both political parties endorsed the referendum and the churches were almost all behind it. There were many people who thought Prohibition was a bad idea but most kept quiet because of the overwhelming public opinion against them. George Storie was not among those people who kept quiet. He was not afraid to let his opinion be known and he was not afraid to take on the Watauga Democrat and its editor, Rob River who was leading the campaign for Prohibition in Watauga County.

This was not the first run-in with the Watauga Democrat and the Prohibitionist. In 1899 an election to ban the making and selling of alcoholic beverages was scheduled to be held in the Blue Ridge Township on August. The voting place was at George Storie's store. The election was never held because of a technicality and many people blamed George Storie for a mix-up that prevented the vote.

In 1906 there was another flare up between the Watauga Democrat and George Storie. George Storie announced that he was a candidate for Watauga County commissioner. On October the Watauga Democrat published the following anonymous letter under the heading "*A Dangerous Candidate: Mr. Editor: we have something of which to complain. We have two good men out for county commissioner. The Republicans have nominated a man out of the Blue Ridge for county commissioner who is an immoral man. He has a gambling machine running in his warehouse. A gang of drunkards lay around him. They drink, play cards and drink right in his house. He is a liquor man from bottom to top. If elected he will do all in his power to fill the county with saloons and his own party is afraid of him as a commissioner.*

The good citizens of this county ought to be informed of this man at once as the people who know him will not vote for him. Clark and Coffey are good men and they should not be beaten by the Liquor King of the Blue Ridge. The county needs sober men to transact its business and don't be afraid to let the people know what kind of man is trying to get hold of the county government." *Citizen* Blowing Rock

The Watauga Democrat gave a rather tepid reply to this letter. They admitted that the letter writer used strong language but did not question any of the charges and pointed out that the writer was a member of George Storie's own party.

However, the people of Aho did not take kindly to outsiders criticizing one of their own. There was a strong sense of community in Aho. A week later the Watauga Democrat printed three letters from leading citizens of Aho defending George Storie's character and refuting the charges made against him by his unknown accuser from Blowing Rock. The first letter was from the teacher at the Aho school, Mr. J. E. Hodges: *"Mr. Editor, the citizen from Blowing Rock whose letter appeared in your last issue has either been misinformed or deliberately makes statements that he cannot substantiate. I have taught two years in the public school almost in Mr. Storie's door. During the school term I have been at Mr. Storie's store as many as two or three times every day and I have never seen any gambling machine or anything that would indicate one. Neither have I seen a drunken man about his store or about his house. In fact, I have never seen a drunken man in this section. I have spent several nights with Mr. Storie and I have never seen anything about his home that would cast reproach on any citizen. In short I have found Mr. Storie, a gentlemen in every particular. I think the county affairs would be safe in his hands. Now let the Citizen from Blowing Rock give his name, come out boldly and substantiates his charges if he can."*

The second letter defending George Storie was from the Rev. James P. Matney, a longtime resident of the Aho section and a legendary Methodist minister in the Blue Ridge section of North Carolina: *"Mr. Editor, I see in your paper of the 18th charges against our Blue Ridge candidate that I think are hardly true. I have known him all his business life and surely if there has been a gambling machine in his house I would have found it out. As often as I have been there I have never seen a gang of drunkards lying around. Mr. Storie like other men is opposed and misrepresented by men who don't like him. He may not be as strictly moral as might be desired. He may not be as strong of temperance as we desire, but I think he is strictly honest, a good neighbor and a good friend to those in need. So let us elect him and see if he don't come out right."*

James Matney and family

The next letter was from Lundy Castle, the granddaughter of Rev. James Matney. Lundy was a teacher and leader in the Friendship Methodist Church: *"Mr. Editor, I have known Mr. Storie for eighteen years. I believe him to be strictly honest. We have patronized his store ever since he has been in the goods business. As far as drunkenness and gambling are concerned I have heard him speak very strongly against it. I have clerked for him much in the past two years. I have neither seen drinking nor card playing. I think Mr. Storie has been very wrongly accused. If there ever was a friend to the needy and to his county, I think Mr. Storie is one."*

LUNDY CASTLE

When the election was held in November George Storie lost. Most of his support came from the Blue Ridge Township. The feud with the Watauga Democrat continued. Apparently George Storie saw a lawyer because on December 21, 1906 The Watauga Democrat received a notice demanding an apology and a retraction of the article called "*a dangerous candidate*" In an editorial the Watauga Democrat danced around the issue: "*Now to the truth of the statements made in said article, this paper never vouched , and immediately extended to Mr. Storie the courtesy of our columns for the purpose of refuting any or all charges made by said correspondent, and which he accepted and in the column of this paper were published three letters from his friends attesting to his good character and standing in the community. This to us seems as least fair. We never at any time intended to treat Mr. Storie unjustly or wrongfully in any respect of manner whatever. That is not the purpose of this paper. Its object is to print the truth, deal honestly with all men, and try to uphold the standards of morality and promote the cause of temperance the very best we can in our feeble way though imperfect it may be, and we shall be guided in the future by the same standards.*

No, Mr. Storie, as before stated we have no intention to do you a wrong or treat you unjustly (and you admitted as much to us) The Editor of this paper was not at all well acquainted with you or your habits, and if we were imposed upon and a wrong was done us, and for the many imperfections of mortal life we stand ever ready to extend apologies."

During the rest of 1907 the feud between the Watauga Democrat and George Storie seemed to have abated. There was no mention of George Storie in the Democrat during the rest of 1907 except for paid ads.

On February 1, 1907 a special session of the General Assembly passed state wide Prohibition law to be ratified by the voters of North Carolina on May 25, 1907. The campaign for the Prohibition law opened a new chapter in the feud between George Storie and the Watauga Democrat.

The first volley in the feud was started by the Watauga Democrat when it made a short notice on March 12, 1908: "*A friend from the Blue Ridge on last Saturday told us that prohibition was rapidly coming to the front in that township. Hurrah for the good people of the ridge."*

George Storie was not slow in answering the Democrat. A week later he wrote a long letter defending his community and letting the county know his opinion on the upcoming prohibition vote: "*Mr. Editor, I notice in your paper of March 12 that a friend told you that the Blue Ridge was coming to the front in the way of prohibition. The Blue Ridge will settle that on May 26th. The people of the Ridge are not ready to sacrifice their liberties through the blood shed by their forefathers who have long since passed away.*

It seems that a lot of people in Watauga think the citizens of the Blue Ridge are a bunch of outlaws but this is not so. They are accused of drinking a lot of whiskey and of being drunkards. I believe there is less drinking on the Blue Ridge than any other township in the county: although we do drink a little whiskey when we can get a little money to order it from other states, our rights are taken away from us in North Carolina.

But while we do drink a little in the Blue Ridge Township we have a better way of controlling it than they have in any other part of the county. If whiskey is at the head of all crimes the county records will show this. Search the records of the county courts and see how many cases on the docket from the Blue Ridge Township; see how many criminal or murder cases you can in Blue Ridge Township since the Civil War.

I served as deputy sheriff under W. H. Calloway for three years but had little business to do. The people all paid their taxes promptly. The first year I collected every cent in the township. I want to say further that there is, no better law-abiding people in the county. To be sure we are going to vote old Blue Ridge wet on the 26th day of May by a large majority.

So let us have our rights and we will all be happy. G. L. Storie"

The following week, Mr. Rivers the editor of the Watauga Democrat wrote an editorial warning the people against the anti- prohibition forces and George Storie: *"Look out voters that you be not deceived by anti-prohibitionist who are lining up for battle. This paper is and has been all the while strictly for prohibition, and while a little surprising, yet the sentiment of the good people of Watauga from every section are placing their talons deep down into the article of Mr. G. L. Storie in last week's issue-aiming at it with a fatal blow that such a doctrine cannot be tolerated by the good people of Watauga County to the ruin of the young men and boys of the county. Therefore it is easy to see from public sentiment, as has been and is being expressed during the week in Boone, that old Watauga will roll up a large majority for prohibition on the 26th of May. But in the meantime it is the duty of every temperance loving citizen in the county to go to work NOW and not to cease until the victory is won."*

The floodgates were open. George Storie became the whipping boy for the prohibition forces and letters poured into the Watauga Democrat condemning the philosophy of George Storie and those who agreed with him. Perhaps the unkindest cut of all came from George Stories twenty-one year old nephew, Thomas Edgar Storie who wrote a letter to the Democrat the following week: *"Will the editor of the Democrat please allow one more article on temperance from the Blue Ridge.*

I have lived in this township for twenty years and I know a little of the influence wielded over its people by the corruptible stuff called whiskey. True as that gentleman said, our people do love their liberties and their freedom. There has been no murdering done within our borders. And, more than this some of our gray headed sires did fight in that great civil war but I believe that the majority of our people do not agree with his ideas on the liquor question. .

Whiskey has certainly worked great harm on our people. It has been the cause of every disturbance in our township as far back as I can remember. Will you voting gentlemen of this township think for one moment of the number of children who are within our township limits and then will you think of the awful influence that this damnable stuff is having over them. The devil is establishing his stamping ground in various parts of this settlement and he is doing it with nothing more than what some of our folks call 'good corn liquor'. If we allow this to go on and do nothing to check it, what will our people come to?

Surely there are men enough in this township who love their country, their children, and their God so well that they can come to the polls and come to the polls and help win one of the greatest victories that North Carolina has ever won.

Now I appeal to you, men, of the good old Blue Ridge, to consider what is before you and go to work for the greatest cause that was ever at stake in our country. Talk temperance at the store, the mill and along the road; and not only do this but in your nightly prayers ask that God will hear and answer prayers to remember us."

There was another unsigned letter form the Green Valley area which poked fun at George Storie's logic: *"I notice in your paper of March 19th a piece from a wet Blue Ridge man claiming that our forefathers fought and died for freedom to drink whiskey, get drunk and kuss and he claims this right has been taken away from us. If this be so ain't it a slam on Satan's kingdom?"*

Another letter from a Mr. Abram Roten, a minister used the Bible as a text to attack the ideas of George Storie: *"I see you have a correspondent who signs his name George Storie who seems to be a great lover of liberty. Wonder if he reads the Bible? One of the first laws God gave us was a prohibition law which prohibited Adam from eating the fruit of a certain tree. Mr. Storie should have done as Adam did.*

My observation has been when a man wants liberty to run over the laws of God and man that he didn't care much for the souls of men who are filling drunkard graves at the rate of one hundred thousand per year. I have been wonderfully pleased with the great tidal wave that prohibition is making in our state and in our nation, but Mr. Storie has taken up his pen and written an illustrious article on lost liberty and the patriotism of the Blue Ridge Township. I fear that prohibition will be lost to the state and maybe the nation, but I venture to assert that lots of good men live in the Blue Ridge Township and will not vote wet with Mr. Storie.

No, Mr. Storie if you were two stories high you could never carry your own township against prohibition. God's hand is in the move and you can't stop it."

There were other letters to the Watauga

Democrat that supported prohibition and condemned George Storie but the message was much the same. By mid-April the tactics began to change. There was a four man committee formed in Boone to support prohibition consisting of two prominent ministers: Reverends J. Brendall and J Davis and two laymen: R. C. Rivers and W. C. Coffey. The purpose of this committee was to hold anti prohibition meetings at the churches in all communities in Watauga County.

The Watauga Democrat did its part by publishing articles from other newspapers advocating prohibition and poems about the effect of liquor on families.

George Storie did not take this sitting down. He placed the following notice in the Watauga Democrat: *"There will be a speaking at the Storie school house in Blue Ridge Township on May 9th by the anti-prohibitionist. Let everyone come and hear something good. We want to tell the prohibitionist how they can have a two month school instead of four as Raleigh has done by voting out the dispensary. So let everyone come and have a good time."*

There is no record of what happened at the gathering at the Aho School. The Watauga Democrat did not report on the activities of the anti-prohibitionist. George Storie was very entertaining speaker so probably many of his friends came to the meeting to hear what he had to say.

The prohibitionist fought back by taking the fight to George Storie's home territory. On Sunday, May 24th two days before the vote on prohibition they scheduled a huge rally sponsored by all four churches in the Blue Ridge Township at Laurel Fork Baptist Church. (Laurel Fork Baptist Church stood on a hill overlooking George Storie's home and business) It was an all-day affair with Sunday school and preaching in the morning, followed by dinner on the ground. In the afternoon there were speeches by Reverends J. Davis and J Brendall, from the prohibitionist committee and short speeches by local people from the Blue Ridge Township who were for prohibition. The grand finale was a speech by Reverend James P. Matney, who was eighty years old and had spent his lifetime opposing liquor of any kind.

The vote on May 26th 1908 was a great victory for the Prohibition advocates in Watauga County and in North Carolina. Prohibition passed by a large majority. Even in the Blue Ridge Township the vote was more than two to one for prohibition. Mr. A. Roten of the Zionsville community had to get in his last digs at George Storie. In a letter to the Watauga Democrat he stated: *"Mr. Editor, please inform Mr. Storie that the cyclone which struck the state, county and Blue Ridge Township was not intended to kill anyone but to give new life and vigor to broken down manhood, made so by whiskey. Now come on all you whiskey men; let make a pull all-together for good home and humanity.*

The star of hope has arisen in the Old North State and we should make it shine brighter and brighter until it shines away all the darkness made by whiskey."

GEORGE STORIE AND THE LENOIR NEWS

After his bitter fight with the Watauga Democrat in 1908, George Storie continued his letter writing campaign against prohibition and other things that offended him but he turned to the Lenoir News which was Republican leaning. Many people in Watauga County especially republicans subscribed to the Lenoir News. It was often read aloud to the patrons of George Storie and Sons Store in Aho.

The first letter George wrote to the Lenoir News was in the summer of 1909 after he and his sons visited Lenoir during the July 4th celebration. The celebration was a big event and George and his sons seemed to have a good time. The next week he penned a letter to the Lenoir New and in the process got in a dig at the Prohibition Law: " *Mr. Editor, I am just home from the celebration in Lenoir and I am not feeling very well. The old woman said I took too much Prohibition but I don't think I did as I only drank one gallon on the trip and that is not enough to hurt anyone. The boys were very much pleased with their trip and the celebration.*

Well, Lenoir certainly did have a nice time. Everything carried out as advertised and everybody was pleased.

We are having fine weather now and the farmers are taking advantage of it. Rye harvesting is on and the crop is good. Corn is looking well and the farmers are putting up the largest cabbage crop in years. Success to the News."

A few weeks later George Storie penned another letter to the Lenoir News. Besides the usual crop report George had to comment on his favorite subject the North Carolina Prohibition Law. *"Editor News, We are having sunshine now and indication of a good hay crop, and crops generally look good excepting fruit due to a late frost.*

I notice that Bristol, Virginia has voted to retain her saloons. I suppose they are tired of sending their money away to build up other towns and cities and decided to keep their money at home and at the same time secure some revenue from the form of license tax from the liquor traffic. I say 'hurray for Bristol'.

It is bad policy to send our money out of the state to build up other communities as North Carolina and other pretend prohibition states are doing."

The next letter that George Storie wrote to the Lenoir News was in defense of one of their suppliers. The owners of the Lenoir Mills (Lutz family) was accused of adulterating the flour it sold by mixing in talc powder.

George Storie wrote:" *To the Lenoir News: We notice in your paper that someone has accused the Lenoir Mills of using adulterations in their flour. We want to say that we have sold untold thousands of pounds of their flour and we can't sell any other flour when we have it. We want to say there is no other flour that is equal to it."*

GEORGE STORIE AND THE GOOD ROADS *MOVEMENT*

George Storie continued his opposition to prohibition but by 1912, it was an established fact in North Carolina and George turned his attention to good roads for the mountain. In this case he was actually supported by the Watauga Democrat. He was an early supporter of the "*Crest of the Blue Ridge Highway*" which was an idea first proposed by the North Carolina State Geologist, Joseph Hyde Pratt. He wanted to build a highway along the Blue Ridge from Tallaugah Falls, Georgia to Marion, Virginia as a means of attracting tourist to the mountain area. George Storie was very interested in building the section that would run from Blowing Rock to Aho. On September 24th 1912 he wrote to the Lenoir News. This letter showed another side of George Storie. He waxed poetically about the beauty of the area. "*Mr. Editor, please allow me space in your paper for a few thoughts which may be of interest of readers of your paper. Most lovers of natural scenery know about Western North Carolina and truly nature has been very lavish in her gifts to the western part of our state. No one traveling from Linville to Murphy will fail to be impressed by the wild and beautiful scenery that everywhere greets the eyes. But I want to speak of a section of the country that has never been opened up to the public because there has been no road that people could travel with any degree of comfort.*

There is a section of country lying between Blowing Rock and Aho which abounds in as varied and beautiful scenery as any part of Western North Carolina. The symmetry of the chain of hills is wonderful and the view from the summit of them is grand. Here the painter can find subjects for his sketches and the poet can find inspiration.

We are now trying to build a road through this section. We want the lovers of nature to become acquainted with it. The road is being built by public labor and contributions and in a short time it will be open so wagons can travel it.

For some time I have been working a force of hands on the road largely at my own expense. When the road is completed we will have a line of roads along the crest if the Blue Ridge from C & O Railroad to Cook's Gap over which an automobile or any other vehicle can travel.

Quite a number of citizens here from Boone, Blowing Rock and Lenoir have contributed to make the road and I want to take this opportunity to thank each and all for their generous contribution."

On July 31st 1914 H. C. Martin the editor of the Lenoir News wrote a front page article in his newspaper that described the road between Green Park to Aho and praised George Storie for his efforts in building the road: *"I recently took a drive over the section of the Crest of the Blue Ridge Highway from Green Park to Aho and to the lover of fine scenery there awaits for the man who has not taken the drive many pleasant surprises.*

The road leads out of the Lenoir to Blowing Rock Turnpike just east of Green Park Hotel and crosses the source of the Yadkin River on a stone bridge near the beautiful spring and passes the grounds of the hotel and winds around Green Hill to the top of the ridge and then follows the top of the ridge to Aho. The road was surveyed by Mr. W. L. Spoon, a noted civil engineer who a few years ago was connected with the good roads department of the United States Government. His position and reputation are a guarantee that the location and the grade are the best possible. As indicated above this five mile stretch of road is to be part of the Crest of the Blue Ridge Highway extending from Virginia to Georgia and it is safe to say that no section of the same length will afford grander or more interesting scenery than this. The construction of the road, like all such undertakings, met with opposition by those interested in other roads and it was only through the efforts of a few men that the road was finally opened to traffic.

    Mr. George Storie, the merchant of Aho was the champion of the good work and through his personal efforts and the contribution of labor and money the road is open.

    It is not finished and much work needs to be done in widening and surfacing but it is in use and affords one of the most pleasant and inviting drive to be had in this region. Mr. Storie is still at work furnishing a team and driver at his own expense. Many public spirited citizens have given Mr. Storie small sums in aid of the work."

In December 1914 George Storie George Storie wrote to the Lenoir New and complained about a number of issues. *"Editor News: well everything is right here in Aho, plenty to eat, plenty to wear. We have to pay the war tax in time of peace, whoever thought of such a thing. The election went off alright. The Republicans one hundred, twenty-three, the Democrats eleven. The Blue Ridge is always right and getting righter every day. Well, what about that six month school the Legislators gave us two years ago. It seems that one month was sidetracked between Raleigh and Greensboro. We only got five months in Watauga this year. The Legislature said we had to have six months schools. The voters of the state said in voting on the amendment this year that they only wanted four months schools. We don't need but four months schools for children from six to twelve years of age. Then we want competent teachers with money to pay them.*

Well, when Brother Davis gets his prohibition campaign before the Legislature this winter it is hoped the ayes and nays will be called for, as our rights and liberties are near enough all taken away.

Well, Christmas will soon be here and I don't think we need to order more than fifty gallons of booze this time as it is hard to get and we have to pay the war tax in times of peace."

Notes: The war tax was passed to make up the loss of tax revenue from European goods entering the country. Part of the tax was on tobacco and alcoholic beverages

In the spring of 1915 George Storie and others were trying to put Aho on the map by building a good road from Darby through Sampson to Aho. This proposed road would have put Boone only eighteen miles from access to a railroad and Blowing Rock only fifteen miles. Major Landon of the Watauga and Yakin River Railroad encourage this road. In August 1915 Wade Harris, editor of the Charlotte Observer made a trip with Major Landon by automobile from Darby to Sampson up the mountain to Aho and on to Blowing Rock. After the trip Wade Harris wrote in the Charlotte Observer that a road from Darby to Aho could be built at a modest cost. The Lenoir News wrote an editorial against the proposed Darby to Blowing Rock road because they knew it would take away from Lenoir the valuable trade with the mountain counties. Of course, the great destruction caused by the great flood of 1916 ended any hope of a good road to Aho which remained a poor and isolated place.

George Storie wrote another letter to the Lenoir News dated March 1, 1915 in which he complained about taxes and prohibition: *"Editor Lenoir News: Please allow me space in your paper. I am living at my place in Penley N. C. Times are hard here. I spent all day last Sunday peeling sassafras bark to get the money to pay the war tax on our little line of drugs that we keep in our store to doctor the babies on. We had to pay a penalty on our tobacco tax of one dollar and twenty cents as we did not have the law and did not get on time. Hard on poor people, but it is Democratic soup and we have to drink it.*

Well I guess the Legislature has passed the anti-jug law stopping the shipment in our state. That is all right, the more prohibition laws we get on the books the more young men will study how to make it. It will add ten blockade stills to one. It was once thought that liquor could not be made in anything but a copper still but that day has passed. It is being made in sourwood logs, pot sheet iron boilers and liquors will still be here when Mr. Davis and his band is dead. Christ made wine at the marriage feast and to be sure it is the best wine that has ever been made but we have got to be better than Christ these days.

Well I shall have to hold up the letter and go on peeling sassafras bark for we have got to pay another tobacco tax on the first of June and it is the only way I have to pay it.

My next letter will be on woman suffrage. I will try to give the fair sex the best showing I can and let them know who get the benefits of it. I will send twenty-five cents of subscription as I like honest men moving along."

The Mr. Davis referred that George Storie referred to in his letter was probably J. F. Davis, a Baptist minister in Boone, Blowing Rock and East Tennessee. Mr. Davis was a well-known fighter for prohibition. In the book, Pilgrims in Paradise, it was stated that: "*Mr. Davis was a fervent prohibitionist and was probably the greatest single influence in voting for prohibition in Watauga County, North Carolina.*"

Unfortunately the letter on women suffrage was never found. The author is sure it would have provided a unique perspective on one of the major issues of that time period.

According to local lore George Storie really enjoyed it when his letters provoked response from other readers of the newspapers. He must have been very happy for he had two strong responses from his March 1915 letter. One was from Wilkes County and the other was apparently from the Aho area signed only as E.A.G. *"In reply to Mr. Storie, Mr. Editor, will you please give me space in your paper for a few words. When I read, Mr. G. L. Storie's piece on tax and prohibition, I could not help thinking of the piece he had written just before Christmas saying the people on the Blue Ridge had plenty to eat and good clothes to wear and they would have fifty gallons of booze for Christmas. I just want to tell Mr. Storie if he will take the money he pays for one gallon of whiskey and pay his war and tobacco tax he won't have to peel sassafras bark to get the money. And by the way Mr. Storie talks, the people down in Penley must have something stronger than Democratic soup to drink. I truly agree with him when he said the whiskey was being made in sheet iron boilers, for when it comes out this way and the men who are used to drinking Democratic soup drink the whiskey, they look very rusty indeed and it must come from a rusty place.*

Now if Mr. Storie will come back to the top of the Blue Ridge and inhale the pure and feel proud that he lives in a prohibition state, I am sure he can pay his war tax without peeling sassafras bark on Sunday."

Another letter was from a man named J. H. Andrews from Wilkes County: *"Editor News, in last week's issue you published a letter signed by G. L. Storie, Penley N. C. in which the writer goes after the Legislature for passing the Anti-jug Law and he stated that the more prohibition laws we have the more liquor we will have and where we have one blockade still we will have ten. Now, Mr. Storie, do you really believe this? Where are all the sheriffs and all officers of the law going to be? Will they disregard their oath of office and shut their eyes to all the violations of the laws of the state? And how about you Mr. Storie: have you ever taken a solemn oath to obey the constitution and laws of North Carolina? And will you sit still and wade around in all this sea of rotten liquor that you say we are going to have because of the anti-jug law? Won't you do your part as a good citizen to uphold the law? If you happen to get on the grand jury will you not report all the violations of the law and fail to do your duty as a good citizen?*

You say you spent last Sunday peeling sassafras bark to pay your war tax. Would it not have been better to spend the Sabbath as some of us did? I spent last Sunday trying to conduct a Sunday school class teaching them to abstain from the use of liquor and tobacco. The prohibition laws will never be too rigid and strict to suit the man who has the good of the rising generation at heart."

Meanwhile George Storie decided to turn over the operation of his store to his sons and moved back to his farm in Sampson (Penley). In 1915 he wrote a letter to the Lenoir New giving the news from his place in Penley and commentaries on the railroad to Darby. *"Mr. Editor, I am now located in Penley while the boys are cutting the rye crop in Aho. We have fine crops in this vicinity, plenty of berries, peaches and some apples. The best work being done in this community is improving our public roads from Aho to Darby. We expect the railroad people will have trains running to Darby in a short time and then we can go to the depot and back in one day and have good roads to travel and no tolls to pay. We can make six trips a week and spend the nights at home with our families.*

Well I have solved the problem of how to reform those two hundred twenty-five fallen women recently discovered in Ashville. Have the government call an extra session of the Legislature and pass another prohibition law forbidding the men from associating with them. Prohibition will stop the lust of the flesh just as easy as it stopped liquor drinking."

The two hundred twenty-five fallen women that George Storie referenced was the number of prostitutes that the city of Ashville found in a survey done in the spring of 1915. Ashville was apparently well known as a place where prostitution was common in the early years of the twentieth century. In an editorial the Lenoir News questioned why the city of Ashville did not survey the number of men who were customers of the prostitutes.

On November 11, 1915, George Storie wrote a letter to the Watauga Democrat, (the first one in years) in his capacity as supervisor of road work for the Blue Ridge Township: *"This is a request that all road supervisors on the different sections of the roads in Blue Ridge Township meet on Thursday, November 25th as is set apart by the president of this great nation. And the good ladies in the various sections are requested to prepare dinner for the hands, a dinner that will do credit to the day, the work in hand, and the men doing it. Hope all other townships will follow."*

The love/hate relationship between George Storie and the Watauga Democrat continued. In November 1917 the Watauga Democrat lauded his efforts to build good roads: *"Mr. George Storie of the Blue Ridge section who by the way is one of Watauga County's good road enthusiasts, was in town Monday. He is very anxious that the link of road between the steel bridge on New River and C. M.* Critcher's Store (on Bamboo Road) *be completed at the earliest day possible and insists that all who are willing to volunteer some work on this much needed road meet him with teams, tools and etc. on Tuesday morning November 27th for the purpose of beginning the much needed work, and we hope people will harken to his call. The work is badly needed and we hope Mr. Storie will succeed in his laudable undertaking of trying to do it with volunteer labor."*

In what may have been his last letter to the Watauga Democrat on February 20, 1919, George Storie complained about all the things that bothered him. He now had national prohibition to complain about: *Mr. Editor, will you please give me space in your paper for a few lines. I see no reference to Captain Lovell and Dr. Little as our representatives. I suppose they are voting for Dog Laws and Prohibition. National prohibition will destroy the greatest industry and the greatest revenue producer. But this is alright. The teachings of Christ at the marriage feast in Galilee and the blood shed by our forefathers from 1776 to 1781 are denied through the prohibition of our government.*

Well, I have a little money that I have gotten through box suppers, that I am going to spend on the roads of the Blue Ridge as we get nothing from the bond money."

After this letter as far as the author can find, the entertaining letters that George Storie wrote to the editor came to an end. His health began to fail. He had what was called then heart dropsy but is now called congestive heart failure. In 1920 G. L. Storie and Sons was dissolved and George bought out the interest of his son Jather Storie, but a year later he sold his store to Jather Storie and son in law, Garfield Church. A year later Jather Storie bought out the interest of Garfield Church.

George and Cad Storie moved back to his home in Aho and his daughter, Maud Crowe moved in to take care of them. He died in 1927.

There is another interesting tale that took place at George Storie's in Aho in April 1913. Dr. Little was in the Blue Ridge area near the store. He heard something and he looked south toward Grandfather a giant hatbox. As it came closer it proved to be an airship with three or four passengers in it. It looked to be about the size of a large wagon.

This airship may have been the source of another tale the author heard from his father that happened when he was a boy. The people who lived in the area near Friendship Methodist Church heard a strange noise that seemed to be coming from the sky. In that time any strange noise especially coming from the sky was thought be the second coming of Christ. The community was terrorized. They gathered together and prayed to await the end of days. Mettie Triplett who lived near the church gathered her children and went across the hill to her mother, Myra Weaver's house. They prayed and waited and watched for the sky to open. Nothing happened and they went on with their lives.

A CIVIL WAR TALE

    A few years ago the author wrote a story about a soldier who deserted the Confederate Army and fled to the mountains and hid out in the hills above Goshen Creek on the Blue Ridge. The story was fiction based on nebulous legends that deserters often hid out in the mountain. However I have discovered a real story about Union men who hid out in the Aho/Bamboo area. The two men were prisoners of war who escaped from a train bound for the living hell of Andersonville in Georgia. The following is their story based on Francis Hosmer's <u>The Story of Andersonville and Other Writings.</u>

    Union soldiers were willing to risk their lives to escape Andersonville Prison in Georgia. By the summer of 1864 everyone in the Union Army was aware that if they were captured and sent to Andersonville that the changes of surviving was not very good. The prison was opened in February 1864 and very soon it was filled to four times its capacity. Food was very scarce and the sanitation at the prison camp was horrible.

    There were one hundred and thirty nine soldiers from the 4th Vermont Regiment captured with Hosmer and Gorham at Reams Station in 1864 and seventy one of them never returned after they were sent to Andersonville.

In 1861 a young men named Francis Hosmer from Vermont enlisted in the Union Army as a musician. In February 1862, another young man, Hiram J. Gorham from St Johnsbury, Vermont enlisted. They were both soldiers in the 4th Vermont Infantry and became good friends. The two served with the Union Army in Virginia in every major campaign from 1862-1864, from Antietam to Cold Harbor. Both men achieved the rank of sergeant.   After the disasters of the battles of Wilderness, Spotsylvania, and Cold Harbor in the spring of 1864, the commander of the Union Army, General Grant tried to out flank the Confederate Army by crossing the James River and capturing Richmond the Confederate capital. The campaign failed to capture Richmond but General Lee's army was bottled up in Petersburg just south of Richmond. The only way General Lee's army could survive was that it was supplied by the Wilmington and Weldon Railroad which was known as the lifeline of the Confederacy. General Grant tried to cut the Wilmington Weldon Railroad which would have probably quickly ended the war.

In June 1864 the 4th Vermont, the military unit in which Hosmer and Gorham served was sent to cut the Wilmington Weldon Railroad six miles south of Petersburg. The raiding party was in the process of cutting the rail lines when they were surrounded and captured by the division of Confederate General Mahone at Ream Station. Hosmer and Gorham were among the prisoners captured.

The prisoners were first sent west to the town of Lynchburg Virginia. From Lynchburg they were marched south toward the railroad at Danville, Virginia. All the Union prisoners knew that they were eventually bound for the dreaded Andersonville. Probably every prisoner was thinking of a way to escape. Hosmer and Gorham were together and they looked for opportunities to escape on the march to Danville but they were guarded too closely. The prisoners spent two nights in a large tobacco warehouse in Danville. On July 4, 1864 six hundred prisoners were loaded on a train bound for Andersonville Georgia. As the train passed through North Carolina at night Hosmer and Gorham discovered a small hole in the side of the rail car that was large enough for a man to slip through. In the dark of the night both men slipped through the hole and jumped. They were not spotted and the train moved on.

H. I. GORHAM.
April, 1864.

Once they were off the train Hosmer and Gorham had to decide where to go to reunite with the Union forces. They decided to go west across the mountains toward Tennessee for two reasons. First they knew that a large part of Eastern Tennessee was controlled by Union forces and they had heard that in Western North Carolina there were many people who sympathized with the Union. Hosmer and Gorham had heard that they could follow the Yadkin River to reach the mountains and then pass through the mountain gaps to reach Tennessee. They headed west hoping to find the Yadkin River. They were very lucky. The first contact they made turned out to be a Unionist family that gave them directions on how to reach the Yadkin River and put them in contact with other Unionists who would shelter them as they followed the river to the west. Often, the only food they found was the blackberries which grew in abundance along the banks of the Yadkin. They were helped by several families with Union sentiment along the Yadkin until they were finally put in touch with a man named Johnson who was leading a group of Confederate deserters and other men trying to avoid conscription. There were over one hundred men in the group and they marched as if they were a military unit. They marched on the road at night and slept in the woods during the day. The group passed through the town of Wilkesboro at night and a few miles past Wilkesboro turned up a tributary of the Yadkin which is now known as Elk Creek. The crude trail crossed the creek many times and led up to what is now known as the Jakes Mountain Road. The Jakes

Mountain Road led to Cooks Gap which was a major gateway into the mountains. As the men slowly made their way up Elk Creek they realized they were being watched. A few days earlier they had passed two women picking blackberries along the banks of the Yadkin. It was later learned that these women tipped off the Confederate authorities that a large group of men were marching toward the mountain. The group was now on Jakes Mountain and getting close to Cooks Gap. Their leader, Johnson found a thicket as a place for the group to hide and he went to the home of Billy Cook, a notorious unionist. Billy Cook let Johnson know that all gaps in that area were being guarded by Confederate home guard. Johnson decided not to return. He set out on his own and was able to cross over into Tennessee. That night, Billy Cook slipped past the guards at Cooks Gap and came to the hideout of the men on Jakes Mountain. He told the men that all gaps going into the mountains were guarded by the Confederate home guard. Hosmer gave the following description of Billy Cook: *"A man of sandy complexion, full beard, about five feet five inches height, a Baptist deacon, fifty-five years of age, of pronounced theological views, and a Union man who had proclaimed his loyalty from the first and who declared that if the Confederacy compelled him to fight he proposed to commence on his own premises."* Billy Cook was the grandson of the original settler in Cooks Gap and knew the area like the back of his hand. He told the men that they were not safe on Jakes Mountain and he guided them to a laurel thicket on Bull Ruffian Mountain near the crest of the Blue

Ridge in the area known as the Storie Settlement. The group of men stayed in this place for several days and Billy Cook gathered food from Union supporters and carried it to them. One day Billy Cook came to the men and told them he had no more food. He advised them to break up into small groups and try to get across the mountains into Tennessee. He told them that some would probably make it but others would be caught. He asked Hosmer and Gorham to stay behind the rest. He told them that his wife was a Storie from the Storie Settlement and wanted to meet some Yankees. (The Storie family was strongly unionist) He took them off the mountain to a hiding place in a laurel thicket near his home in Cooks Gap. That night Eliza Storie Cook came to Hosmer and Gorham's hiding place bringing them their supper. She sat and talked long into the night. She told them of all the privations the mountain people faced during the war. She told them that she had not had a match in her house for two years and that she had broken her last needle a year ago so she could not do her sewing. Hosmer gave her a needle from his soldier's sewing kit. Mrs. Cook told them about her family who lived in the Storie Settlement. She told them she had three brothers in the war. One had died in camp in Virginia, another was missing after the battle of Missionary Ridge and the other joined the Union Army in Tennessee. She told them about her sister and cousin who carried food to deserters who hid out in the mountains.

The next day a storm was threating and Billy Cook came and took the two men to an apple cellar under his corn crib where they spent the night. Early the next morning Billy Cook went to the apple cellar with their breakfast and told them he had seen tracks of men near his house which he believed was the home guard. (The leader of the home guard in eastern Watauga County was Lieutenant John Hartley who owned the farm next to Billy Cook's farm. John Hartley's wife, Eunice was a first cousin to Billy Cook)   It began to rain hard later that morning. At midmorning, Eliza Cook came to the corn crib in a very agitated state. She told Hosmer and Gorham that the home guard had just left their house with Billy Cook in custody. The two men knew they had to leave quickly.
They bade Eliza Cook a hasty goodbye and headed across the nearby creek and headed out in a southern direction in heavy rain. They soon became lost in woods not able to tell direction. They finally found a blazed trail (cuts made in trees to indicate direction) and followed it because they had no other clue on where to go. They followed it for about five miles when they came to an opening in the woods. As Hosmer and Gorham entered the clearing they heard the clicks of rifle hammers and the command "halt". They had walked into the middle of a home guard camp.

Hosmer and Gorham were taken as prisoners to an old house nearby. As they were marching there the guards told them they had a prisoner who they probably knew. They suspected it was Billy Cook. When they got to the old house they were separately taken to Billy Cook and asked if they knew him. Both men denied that they had ever seen Billy Cook knowing that he would probably be shot as a traitor if they admitted that he had helped them. That night the two men were put in a room with Billy Cook and watched but they made no indication that they knew each other.

The next day the prisoners were marched to Boone and lodged in the jail there, an old log building of four rooms. In one of the rooms was lodged the Storie girls (Elizabeth and Lucy) who had been arrested about the same time as Billy Cook. Hosmer gave one of the girls a small silver Greek cross, the badge of his Vermont division.

The next day the prisoners were gathered together to prepare them for a march to Morganton about forty miles away. There was no regular ropes available in Boone so a rope was made from withes from hickory saplings and Hosmer and Gorham were tied together. The march took two days. When they reached the prisoner of war camp in Morganton they found that about half of the men who marched up Yadkin and up to Cooks Gap with them had been captured. Billy Cook was also with them. Hosmer and Gorham were able to talk freely with him. He fully expected to be shot as a traitor. It was not until many years later that they learned that he survived the war and died an old man.

Hosmer was put on trial because someone accused him of being Johnson, the leader of the group of one hundred, thirty-two men who trying to cross the mountains into Tennessee. He was able to prove his innocence.

After a few days Hosmer and Gorham were sent to Salisbury and from there to Andersonville. They were lucky. They survived Andersonville and were freed at the end of the war.

In 1906 Hiram Gorham paid a visit to Boone and told the Watauga Democrat of his experiences as an escaped prisoner of war in Boone in 1864. He was living in New York at the time. He did not see anyone he remembered from 1864. He was very surprised that the wilderness land he saw during the Civil war was in 1906 prosperous farm land.

In June 1920 Hiram Gorham paid another visit to Boone. He was then a very old man and a resident of the Old Soldiers Home in Johnson City, Tennessee. He visited in the home of W. L. Bryan who was a member of the Watauga Home Guard and witness to some of the events described in the Hosmer book.

BOONE COFFEY AND HIS SISTERS

Boone Coffey and his family moved to the Blue Ridge settlement soon after the end of the Civil War. They came from the Mulberry section of Caldwell County which is at the foot of the Blue Ridge Mountains. No one knows why a black family would choose to live in a backwoods mountain community. Maybe it was because the Blue Ridge settlement was known for its unionist sentiments. The Coffey farm was over three hundred acres which was the largest farm in the Blue Ridge settlement. There are a number of theories about how ex slaves acquired so much land. One theory says it was a gift from their former owner. Wyimeth Bradshaw Jenkins recalled that her mother said that two of the Coffey sisters worked for some wealthy people and earned enough money to buy the farm. Land was dirt cheap in the years after the Civil War and much of the Coffey farm was considered useless for farming. The Coffey family was first listed in the federal census of 1870. Solomon Coffey, age fifty-nine and his wife Lucy, age fifty-nine were listed as former slaves. Five children were listed: Louise, age twenty-eight, Sarah age twenty-six, Liza age twenty-four, Boone age twenty-one, Jones age eighteen, and Lewis age sixteen. Local legend says that Jones Coffey went to Idaho and may have helped the financially. Anna Teague Canipe recalled that here grandmother; Greene would write letters to Jones that Liza would dictate. Solomon and Lucy died soon after they moved to the Blue Ridge.

In August 1897 the French Broad Hustler had the following item concerning the Coffey family: *"the Blue Ridge Township is honored with one colored taxpayer who lists one billy goat and $44 dollars in cash. One devout old gentleman told the list taker that he had no money to give in this year: that he had given it all to the Lord. His money is said to be in the bank and the county commissioners will investigate. When they get to lying on the Lord it is time to call a halt."*

The Lenoir Topic on January 30th 1884 had the following article: *"One night last week Calvin Underwood and Boone Coffey went hunting on the Yadkin and denned two foxes and caught them, treed two wild cats up a tree, cut the tree down and got the cats and found the tree was a bee tree rich with wild honey. They say it was not an extra good night for hunting either."*

Boone Coffey was well known as a hunter. He rode a big black horse and his pack of hounds followed him. Wyimeth Bradshaw Jenkins remembers that Boone came to her daddy's blacksmith shop in Sampson to have his horse shod. Boone was very proud of his dogs. In 1917 there was a note in the Lenoir News that stated: *"Mr. Boone Coffey had lost a dog and I fear he will go crazy if someone doesn't find it for him."*

A common practice in Aho at that time was to exchange work with neighbors. The Coffey family often exchanged work with the Lawson Kerley family which lived on the other side of the mountain from the Coffey farm.

John Hawkins tells that Boone would often come to visit in Buffalo Cove and stay several days. He said that everyone called him "Uncle Boone". Len Cottrell of Laytown said that Boone would often visit his family and the boys would fight over who got to sleep with him.

Another story related by John Hawkins that a man named Elijah Coffey (no relation) was very sick in bed. Boone Coffey came by and asked Elijah if he wanted to go hunting. Forgetting about his illness, Elijah jumped out of bed, put on his clothes, called his dogs and he and Boone set out for the hills.

Dean Hatton Barber recalls that Boone courted his aunt, Belle Hatton. Boone always came courting in a three piece suit with a gold chain. However the romance must have hit a snag. Belle married another man and Boone remained a bachelor for the rest of his life.

Many people believe that Eliza worked as a nurse for a wealthy California silk merchant and when she returned to the farm in Aho she brought with her two trunks full of silk cloth. Sarah and Eliza always dressed in silk. They attended church at Laurel Fork Baptist and always were dressed to the nines. They sat in the back pew of the church.

Sarah died of exposure in 1923 when she became lost in the mountain while pulling galax. Eliza died of a stroke in 1927. The farm was sold to Hub Stuart but Boone was still allowed to live there. The people of Aho helped take care of Boone after he became disabled. He died in 1931.

Joe Greene of the Aho community built coffins for Boone and his two sisters. They were buried in the Storie Family Cemetery located between milepost 288 and 289 on the Blue Ridge Parkway. There are four graves separated from the other graves in the cemetery marked only with fieldstones. The author is not sure who is buried in the fourth grave.

Boone Coffey in his old age his cane and doorstep

THE CHURCHES IN AHO

The first settlers in Aho had to go to Three Forks Baptist Church on the South Fork of the New River. By 1855 there was enough people for the Storie and Greene families to build their own Baptist Church and named it Laurel Fork. After the Civil War a number of people who were members of the Northern Methodist Church moved into the Aho area. Sometimes in the late 1870's these families built Friendship Methodist Church.

On February 27, 1889 The Watauga Democrat had this article about Laurel Fork Church: *"Brother E. F. Jones visited the Laurel Fork Church last Monday, Tuesday and Wednesday and preached with Brother Gragg. The brethren fell in love with brother Jones. They seemed to be surprised that he could preach so. They say he has been badly misrepresented to them. They say they want him to visit them again as soon as he can."*

The first notice about Friendship Church was in the Watauga Democrat in July 1890. The newspaper reported that the quarterly meeting of the Methodist Episcopal Church North was held at Friendship Methodist Church. Elder Cannon and Pastor Smith conducted the meeting.

In July 1894, Mr. G. H. Harstin wrote a letter to the Watauga Democrat about the community of Aho. He moved to Aho sometimes after the Civil War became a respected citizen and a leader in Friendship Methodist Church. Mr. Harstin wrote: *"Farmers are very busy battling sheep sorrel, Johnson grass etc. Oats are looking finely and corn is looking well considering past weather. Our Sabbath Schools are good in this community. Laurel Fork Church has seventy names enrolled, and is well attended. Friendship Church has thirty names enrolled. They are having a good school and there is life in it.*

I had the pleasure of visiting a Sabbath school concert at Friendship Church last Sabbath gotten up by Miss. Jenny Matney and Mrs. M.C. Shull which proved to be a grand success. The church was beautifully decorated with evergreens and the children wore bouquets and wreaths of roses. A large crowd gathered. The program was very much enjoyed by the audience. All the pieces by the girls and boy were admirably rendered. But we must not forget to mention the little ones which have been under the instruction of that experienced and Christian teacher, Miss Jenny Matney. The part they took in the exercises proved that they were well trained in Sabbath school."

Reverend K. L. Haga was a well-known evangelist in the Northern Methodist Church. On August 21, 1910 he conducted a very successful revival at Friendship Methodist Church. He was assisted by aged local minister James P. Matney known as Uncle Jimmy. During the thirteen days Mr. Haga preached twenty-five sermons and Mr. Matney preached one.

The Watauga Democrat usually did not cover revivals in detail but this was very important meeting and on September 21, 1910 it wrote: *"Sunday morning dawned bright and clear and the people began coming early. The song service began at 10:30 and the choir did excellent work for 30 minutes and then the sermon began. To a crowded house which gave great interest, a sermon lasting 40 minutes was preached from the subject of 'the eyes that see everywhere' and on Sunday night another interesting service was held and the house was filled to the utmost capacity, both seating and standing room being occupied. The subject was "The Prodigal's Return.' The meeting was continued until Friday. The people say this meeting is the best for years in this part of the country. Many young men who wandered off in sin returned and gave their heart to God. The house of worship was a place of happiness at every service. The meeting closed on Friday night. Eleven persons united with the church and received baptism."*

Friendship Methodist Church joined the Boone Methodist Circuit in 1939 when the Northern and Southern branches merged. The Reverend Paul Townsend delivered the first sermon on November 5th.

There was an important meeting of the Stony Fork Baptist Association at Laurel Fork Baptist in September 1897. Churches from all over western North Carolina were represented. The Watauga Democrat reported that it was: *"very pleased with our Blue Ridge friends. They are kind and hospitable and improving in many ways. It was also noted that there was some applejack but it did not disturb the solemnity of the occasion."*

Everything went well until a delegate from Caldwell County spoke. He spoke about education in the mountains and he used the fact that the people of the Blue Ridge recently vote against a school tax as a pretext to attack them. He made the charge that most of the mountain people were: *"were ignorant and kept a horseshoe over their door and the women kept a flint rock in the fireplace to keep the hawks from catching chickens."* This remark angered many of the delegates from the mountains and some of the local people wanted to take the Caldwell delegate out and hang him to the nearest tree, but cooler heads prevailed.

A few weeks earlier at the Brushy Fork Baptist Church west of Boone another meeting was not so congenial. A wild rabble of whiskey men camped out near the church where they caroused, drank and sold whiskey. They even attacked some of the young men who attended the meeting at the church using brass knuckles. The Watauga Democrat wrote an editorial demanding that laws against disturbing worship be enforced.

1997 must have been the year for verbal attacks on the people of the Blue Ridge. Earlier in the year a preacher from Elkin, North Carolina, Reverend C. W. Robinson wrote that along the Blue Ridge from Blowing Rock to the Virginia line there was a ten mile wide area where there were no churches or schools. He said that the people of this area were very:" *destitute, heathenish, and ignorant."*

Some of the things the minster said were patently false. Almost every community had a church and most had a one room school. However many parents did not send their children to school. They did not see the need for education and believed the children were needed to work on the farm.

On January 28, 1909 the Watauga Democrat printed a letter by an anonymous person praising the pastor at Laurel Fork Baptist, J. M. Payne. *"I wish to say there has been one of the most wonderful revivals of religion at this church we have ever witnessed. It began of Sunday night January 10th and closed on Thursday January 21th. There was large attendance at each service, the very best of behavior, and the preaching was almost unequaled with the result of twenty two additions to the church. The pastor is now rewarded for his faithfulness and we are glad to state that the people of Aho contributed liberally to his financial needs—about $23 and some produce which others intend to give.*

Aho now ranks as high as any other community in the county morally, religiously and otherwise, but we attribute the highest honor to religion as religion promotes love and good among men, lifts the head that hangs down, heals the wounded spirit, dissipates sorrow, sweeten the cup of affection, and blunts the sting of death."

Friendship Methodist Church 1940
The lady on the left is Annie Castle and
On the right Lundy Castle (others unknown)

The earliest photo I could find of Laurel Fork
Baptist Church probably made around 1900.

Friendship Methodist Church congregation 1900
Many local people can be identified in this photo.

THE SAMPSON COMMUNITY

It was a common practice to burn the brush on the land where timber had been cut and then plant corn on the burned over area. The ashes from the burning brush would fertilize and sweeten the acidic soil. In the spring of 1891 two brothers, John and Wilborn Turnmire spent the day burning off a new ground on the Turnmire farm on Joes Fork Creek in Sampson. They watched the fire until late at night and decided it was safe to take a rest. The tired John lay down and soon fell asleep. When John woke up his brother was gone. He searched for his and some distance away he found his brother lying in a bed of coals, dead. Wilborn's body was horribly burned. It was not known if he fell into the fire or passed out from the falling sickness (epilepsy) before he fell into the fire. It appeared that Wilborn died without a struggle. The next day his funeral was held at Sampson Baptist Church and he was buried at the local cemetery. After the burial, rumors began to spread casting suspicion on Wilborn's brother, John. The rumor was that there was bad blood between the brothers and that Wilborn's head had been crushed. Wilborn's uncle, L. G. Turnmire swore out a warrant accusing John of murdering his brother. The Watauga County coroner went to Sampson and ordered the body which had been buried for two weeks, disinterred for examination. The body was examined by the coroner and Dr. Reece. No fracture of the skull was found and no violence that might have caused death was discovered.
However, the jury rendered a verdict against John Turnmire because they believed a full investigation

of all the circumstances was needed.

D. B. Dougherty, Justice of the Peace went to Sampson and conducted a hearing. After examining the states witness the Justice of the Peace dismissed the charges.

Another tragedy took place in Sampson in March 18th, 1914 when an eighteen year old boy, Frank Triplett was out hunting and dropped his gun. The gun went off killing young Frank and setting his clothing on fire. The fire also spread to the woods. The fire alarmed the neighbors, but before anyone could reach him the body was burned beyond recognition.

Another incident happened at the Sampson Baptist Church in the summer of 1891. A group of young planned to disturb the services at the church. The result was a general melee with the preacher taking flight. Justice of the Peace, Dougherty held a hearing at Aho and questioned thirty witnesses. He charged four men, Jesse Adams, Tim Robbins, Jerry Storie and L. L. Jones with disturbing religious services and bound them over to court.

The trial of the four men was held on October 15, 1891. They were found guilty and their

sentences were graded by the severity of the offense. Jesse Adams was sentenced to sixty days, Tom Robbins to forty days, Jerry Storie to thirty days and L. L. Jones to twenty days in jail.
When the timber was mostly cut in Sampson most people moved away. During the prohibition it was an ideal place for bootleggers and moonshiners. In fact there were so many stills in Sampson that moonshiners were reporting on each other. The Lenoir News Topic reported in May 1930 that revenue officers destroyed a still on Dugger Creek that rival moonshiners had reported to them. They poured more than four thousand gallons of beer into Dugger Creek and forty-five gallons of moonshine whiskey was seized. The lookout on the top of Dugger Mountain fired warning shot and the operator fled into the woods but still was still running when the revenue officers arrived.

THE DEATH OF ELISHA HOLDER

A common occupation in the late 19th century was the traveling cobbler. Elisha Holder from the Blue Ridge community in Watauga County supported his wife Nancy and young son, Frank Holder by traveling near and far as a traveling cobbler. He would visit a home with his equipment and usually using a beef hide that the family had tanned he would measure and cut out shoes for each member of the family. A small family would take a couple of days and a large family would take a week or more. There were a number of travelling cobblers in Watauga County so Elisha Holder had to travel into Tennessee to find homes where he could pry his trade.

In the summer of 1876 Elisha set out for Tennessee to pay the property tax on land he owned there. He went up Stone Mountain on the Old State Road. He walked with his pack until near dark when he stopped to camp for the night. He was less than a mile from Bakers Gap.

There was another man on the Old State Road that night. His name was Frank Gillum, who was well known desperado in Eastern Tennessee and Western North Carolina. He was always on the lookout for easy prey. Elisha Holder offered to share his merger fare with Frank Gillum. Elisha also shared with Gillum that he had come to Tennessee to pay the taxes on the land he owned there. Gillum, thinking Elisha had money hit him over the head and took his money pouch. However Elisha had already paid his taxes and was on his way back home.

On July 15, 1876 The Caldwell Messenger wrote: *"Mr. J. L. Moretz: A man was found dead on the Old State Road ¾ miles from Bakers Gap on the Tennessee side. The head was off the body and the pants and boots were missing. It was later learned that the body was of Elisha Holder of Watauga County. The remains were so decomposed that the cause of death could not be ascertained but we hear that a negro and white man have been arrested under suspicion."*

The remains of Elisha Holder were found by Major James Miller. Apparently the two men who were arrested had an alibi because no one was charged in the murder.

Meanwhile, Frank Gillum went to Blowing Rock and went on a stealing binge. J. W. Sudderth led a posse that arrested Gillum and recovered the stolen property. Frank Gillum was taken to jail in Boone. Just how Gillum got out of jail is unknown. He continued his career of robbing and killing for another twenty years. Finally, twenty one years later Frank Gillum's career of crime came to an end. He was hanged for his crimes somewhere in Tennessee. On the gallows he confessed to killing five men among them Elisha Holder. He remembered killing Holder for his money and finding only forty-five cents. He also stated that he carried off the old man's satchel but finding nothing in it he left near the home of Arch Thompson.

On May 31 Roy and Robert Holder grandsons of Elisha Holder went to Stone Mountain Tennessee to find the grave. The following is Robert Holder's account of the trip: *Mr. Roby Shull who is about eighty and Jake Hodges who is in his sixties took us to the place where the crime took place some ninety six years ago. Mr. Shull seemed to know more about this than anyone I have talked with. He said the man was hanged in Kentucky (other sources say Tennessee) for murdering someone else but confessed on the gallows to murdering Grandfather Holder. This place is not far from Mountain City. It is very rough and rugged country. The last mile is very rough and can only be reached in a four wheel drive.*

According to Mr. Shull's statement there was a small cast iron cooking pot and a galvanized pan about nine inches in diameter and three inches deep hanging in a rhododendron bush at the scene of the murder. Mr. Shull said it belonged to the old man (Elisha Holder). He stated it had been there as long as he could remember. It was nailed to a pine tree for many years until the nail rusted away and he showed us the spot on the tree where the nail had been. After the nail rusted away someone hung them in the laurel bush where they have grown into the wood. Evidently they have been there many years. I closely observed this."

Robert Holder

BITS AND PIECES FROM THE WATAUGA DEMOCRAT FROM AHO, SAMPSON AND BAMBOO

The first reference the author found when the name Aho was used was in the Lenoir Topic dated January 24, 1888. It was signed by Buffalo Bill a named often used as a pseudonym for someone writing to the local newspaper. The author used fake biblical language to chastise those who rejoiced that the Watauga Journal ceased publishing. There is no clue to the person who wrote it. The author wrote: *"Any man can strike a dead lion, or play with the heels of a dead colt but it takes a brave man to beard a living lion or tickle the heels of a living colt. He that mocketh the dead has his reward and he shall gather tribute from the people until there is no more tribute then shall his end come and the people shall mock at his calamity."*

Taylor Greene was Civil War veteran who lived on the Blue Ridge in the Bamboo area. After the war he married Harriet Newell Adams Storie, the widow of Noah Storie. On March 11, 1897 he was visiting his sister in law, Charity Greene in the Globe. He was sitting in a chair and fell dead of a heart attack.

On April 10, 1903 Mrs. Alice Craig locally famous for operating a disorderly house (whore house) on the Aho Road entered one hundred acres of land on the waters of Middle Fork Creek. It is assumed that it was the steep mountain behind her house reaching toward the crest of the Blue Ridge.

Myra Hartley Weaver was born in Bamboo and moved to Aho when she married John Weaver. She lived to be 100 years old. In another book the author quoted an interview she gave the Lenoir News Topic when she was ninety-eight years old.. In the Lenoir News in 1901 there was a letter about her grandmother and namesake Myra Norris Cook, who was an ancestor of many people in Aho and Bamboo, from her daughter B. F. Tester: *"This author is now living with Myra Cook who is 85 years old; and has raised 18 children. She had 131 grandchildren and 109 great grandchildren and has children in five states. She never used tobacco, took medicine nor used liquor in her life and can see how to sew, knit and read without the use of glasses. She is able to walk several miles to visit her neighbors and is enjoying good health at this writing."*

It was an important job of the sheriff and his deputies to go to the townships and collect the property taxes. Notices were put in the paper that on a certain day the sheriff would be a specified location to collect the taxes. This was a golden opportunity for thieves. In April 1894 Deputy Sheriff Hampton who was from the Blue Ridge was sent to Blackberry to collect some tax money. As he crossing the Blue Ridge near the John Ford place he was accosted by two men unknown to him with pistols drawn. They took thirty dollars and fled down the mountain toward Blackberry.

In the days before social security many old people were left on their own. It was especially hard for widows and old maids. The churches and the men of the community in Aho were very generous in helping these people. The Watauga Democrat on February 1, 1916 had the following notice: *"The spirit of Christmas seems to linger among us. During and since the holidays the men of the community visited the homes of Aunt Minerva Canter, Miss Malinda Weaver, Mrs. Julia Castle and Mrs. J.P. Matney and left a bountiful supply of wood at each place. Who says the men of Aho are selfish? I don't believe it."*

On June 24th 1920 The Watauga Democrat reported that John Keller was crushed to death when a sled loaded with tan bark turned over on him. He was driving down a steep mountain road when his team of horses ran away. It is thought that he had been dead for more than an hour when he was found. He was a thrifty, energetic citizen. He left a young wife and a baby boy.

The community of Bradshaw no longer exists. In the years after Second World War the families that lived in the area between Penley and the Richlands moved away. The building that served as the church and school was closed. However in the 1930's the school was an active place. In 1934 the Lenoir News Topic gave the following account of a Halloween party that took place in 1934: *"Last Wednesday our teacher Miss. Wyimeth*

Bradshaw gave us a Halloween party at the school house. The party was given to us because we raised our standards of reading both silently and orally. Fortunately every student received an invitation to the party which was given in the form of a tacky party. The invitations were written in green ink on yellow and orange paper. With the invitation each child was given a ticket to hand to the witch at the door before they could enter. The floor was strewn with various colors of autumn leaves and the spooky looking bats, cats, witches and owls added a note of beauty as well as simplicity to the room. Many games were played such as Blind Fold, Pussy want a Cornet, and Poor Pussy. Follow each game was a contest in which each student was allowed to take part. Prizes were won by Ilene Storie, Mastin Bradshaw, Milton Greene, Rhonda Bradshaw and Myrtle Storie. After the games and contest the witch led the children to a table covered with orange paper with a jack-o-lantern as the centerpiece. The children found their places by the different designs placed on the table cloth border. The refreshments consisted of cakes, candy and cocoa. Gene Storie 8th grade"

The Bradshaw Baptist Church and school house around 1900. The school closed about 1940.

There was another incident at the church about 1940. There was a box supper at the church and people came from all around the area. Someone from Blowing Rock came probably to see one of the Bradshaw girls. He drove a beautiful 1935 Ford Roadster. When he came out all four tires had been cut. It was rumored that the person who cut the tires was a Ford from Aho.

PICTURES

The Aho school house. The people in the picture are Annie Castle, Della Crow, Exie Crow, Cleota Crow and Agnes Storie.

Milking Time at the Weaver farm 1945

The cattle are gathered at the gap waiting to be milked. William Weaver and his cousin Buddy Hollars are mounted on Prince and Maud, good and faithful servants for many years.

This was a going away party for Ashbury Weaver in May 1918 when he went into the U. S. Army. The place is old Weaver home. The time of the year can be identified by the blooming snowball bushed in the background. The following people can be identified in the picture: first row, boy unknown, Squire Greene, Omi Triplett, Myra Weaver, Amanda Weaver Greene, Callie Triplett, Mary Triplett, Melinda Weaver, second row, unk, unk, Erwin Hollars holding child, Mamie Weaver Hollars, Mettie Weaver Triplett, unk, Bob Triplett, unk, Eugene Day, Ella Weaver Day, Ruth Weaver Castle, Ashbury Weaver, Cassie Hampton, unk, Spencer Storie, third row, unk, Marion Coffey, unk, Eliza Weaver, unk, Jesse Triplett, unk, unk.

THE END

Made in the USA
Charleston, SC
07 December 2015